THE POWER OF A MAN

THE GOOD, THE BAD, THE BROKEN
ONE WOMAN'S PERSPECTIVE THROUGH POETRY

GENEISE FULLER

FOREWORD BY TERRY J. DRAKE

Copyright © 2020 GeNeise Fuller

All rights reserved. No part of this book may be reproduced or used in any manner without the prior written permission of the copyright owner, except for the use of brief quotations in a book review.

To request permissions, contact the publisher at info@enterpromedia.com

Paperback: 978-0-578-73553-5

First paperback edition August 2020

Edited by Brinkley Fuller
Cover art by Brinkley Fuller
Layout by Brinkley Fuller
Photographs by Charles Pruitt
Photographs by GeNeise Fuller

Printed by Enterpromedia in the USA.

Enterpromedia
Birmingham, AL

www.enterpromedia.com

What is man that You are mindful of him,
And the son of man that You visit (give attention to or care for) him?
For You have made him a little lower than the angels,
And You have crowned him with glory and honor.
You have made him to have dominion over the works of Your hands;
You have put all *things* under his feet.
Psalm 8:4-6 (NKJV)

INTRODUCTION

This book of Poetry is designed to Honor, Challenge, and Support one of God's Most Valuable Creation, MEN.

I Honor you Men, because you are an Awesome Creation. God, created you FIRST, and That carries weight, value, and a huge responsibility! You were made to handle it! That is why you were first and I Honor You.

I Challenge you with the responsibility of First, to take care of God's women and children. You are to Cover them, Protect them, and Love them. You are Not to Abuse them, Harm them, or Kill them. Love and Life is given by God. I challenge you to honor that.

I Support you. As being the First and the Head, things don't always come together as planned. Not only do I support, but I believe in You, Men and I am not alone. I speak for a lot of women who understand life isn't always easy. There will be times of brokenness, sorrow, heartaches and even disappointments. Let's be honest, no one is immune from these things. Our love and support are with you because we believe in You!

DEDICATION

This book is dedicated to MEN everywhere and the Women and Children who love them.

FOREWORD

In the beginning, God asked Adam this question, "Where are you?" I often wonder how frequently God has asked this same question throughout generations. I believe the same question is currently being asked by society, by women, and unfortunately by our children with few men willing or able to give a reply. The search for men has taken us on a journey throughout the corridors of life, searching high and low for men to give an account of where they are. Not only has society, women and children been looking for men, but the creator of life as well. In Ezekiel 22:30, we see God expressing his utter disappointment in not finding one.

The search for men has left a gamut of emotions. It has some pondering in their minds, some abandoning the search, and some with heads hung low, who are painfully trying to fight off the forceful reality that there may be no hope in finding who they are looking for. Before we walk off in utter hopelessness, GeNeise has penned a series of heart wrenching poems that must get into the hands of men across the world. Whether they are at the bar, the ballpark, the bowling alley, the church, or in their secluded man-cave, we must get this book to them with a sense of urgency. Our families, our communities, our cities, our states depend on men wrestling with the thought-provoking poetry that rests on these pages. I believe these poems will jolt the minds of every man who will accept the challenge of picking up this book. In doing so, the book will cause a forever change in the trajectory of their life.

When we find the location of men, we will see that the boy grew into an adult, but somewhere on his journey lost the power that belongs to a man. There are men who stepped into adulthood but were never mentored to recognize and develop the power he possesses. Due to this truth, today we have men who are not living the powerful, prolific, potent, and purposeful life that he was intended to live. Instead they have settled for everything but possessing the power of a man. So, it is time that men take a look in the mirror and be confronted with their good, their bad, and their broken states to find healing and solutions. Then they will be more than capable to answer the question, "where are you?"

GeNeise has accepted the challenge to boldly walk through the highly defended barracks that lie in the mind of men to offer solutions that will reconnect them to their power source. In doing so, men can rise and be who they were purposed to be and to walk in the power that was theirs all along.

Men, I challenge you not to just look at this book as a book of poetry, but look at this book as a plea and request from the heart of one woman saying, "men, we need you and here is help."

Terry J. Drake, Pastor

TABLE OF CONTENTS

The GOOD   13
The Power of A MAN
My HERO
Why are You So Good to Me? (You ask)
Gentleman of The WORD
The Power of Your Presence, MAN
The Power of Touch
Let Me Love You Right
Happy Father's Day – Man of God
SHE WOULD BE SO PROUD
The Power of CHOICES

The BAD   27
Where Are You? (A message to Dads)
Where Are They? (Con't Message to Daddies)
You See Me, As a Strong Black Women
What happened to You?
Let My Sister Go!
And Now, You Wanna Come Back?
Who Gave You The Right?!
The Power of Touch (the Other side)
REALLLY???
If Black Lives Matter

The BROKEN   44
Who, will MENtor them?
Save Our Men
Why Didn't He Leave?
Beneath the Smile
UnWanted Child
God, will You talk to my daddy for me?
Fed-Up!
Black Men DO Cry
Encouraging the Man I Love
Lord, Teach him How to Love Me

The SOLUTION?   **62**
But what about, your word?
It's Hell being a Trailblazer
The Power of YOU!
Will You be **THE** One?
It Only Takes One
The Power of Influence
Excuses
I'll Make it Worth Your While
Prayer for Direction

The AFTERWORD   **78**
The AUTHOR   **80**

The POWER of A MAN

POWER (in a person) is the ability to influence or change an outcome.
Source: study.com

The GOOD

(noun) **That which is morally right; righteousness**
Source: Google.com

The POWER of A MAN
GeNeise Fuller – Author/Poet

STRONG! SECURE! SEXY!
WITTY! WISE! Not messy

COMPETENT! CONFIDENT! COMPLETE!
ADMIRABLE! ADORABLE! Gives up his seat

BEAUTIFUL! BRAVE! BOLD!
HANDSOME! HANDY! And much more to be told

You may read this and say
Girl, what man is this?
Or, where is he?
Is this the one I missed?

I found, if you look closely
Some of these attributes you will see
Or, if you look with your eyes of Faith
You can decree these things to be

I definitely believe
In the Power of a Man
Especially, if he's Godly
And has placed his life in God's hands

The sky is beyond limits
In what this man can do
With the Respect, Honor and Praise
That will beam from you!

So, celebrate that man
God has placed in your life
And you will be Amazed
Seeing your Love reach new heights!

MY HERO

GeNeise Fuller – Author/Poet

You make me so proud
I want to shout it aloud!

MY HERO, My Love
Sent from above

You are a Great Father,
Husband and Lover
You are MY HERO
There 'ain't' no other!

Handsome, **E**xciting, so thankful you're mine!
Romantic? Yes! And **O**h so kind.

Happy, is what you have made me
Forever grateful baby, I will be.

Can I tell you, just one more time?
You are MY HERO, My Love
SO glad you're mine! ❤©

Why are You So Good to Me?
(You ask)

GeNeise Fuller – Author/Poet

Why are you so good to me?
Why would I not be good to you?

I Love you. I honor you
And respect you as my man
You are kind, lovable
Hard working and understands

For your family
Your love runs deep
You show care and concern
For everyone you meet

Especially the children
And the elderly too
That is why the good
Is returned unto you

You are strong, yet gentle
You are funny, yet wise
Why would I not be good to you?
You make me feel So alive!
I Love You

Gentleman of The WORD

GeNeise Fuller – Author/Poet

Always a gentleman, a true brother
Doing all you can to help others

Reaching inside to share your last
Ignoring the critics of your past

Analyzing your steps as you move ahead
Not shaken by life because you're Jesus led

Honoring the Father with your heart
On point with His love that never departs

Realizing your life was designed, to give God glory,
Now you can finally share your story

Of how Eternal life is a Great gift from God
And that others can have a brand new start.

The Power of Your Presence, MAN

GeNeise Fuller – Author/Poet

Your influence, either Good or Bad
Can have a profound impact upon a little Lad

Whether young, old, female or male
The Power of Your Presence is about to be unveiled

You were chosen by The Almighty to be The Head
Wow! What an Honor, this is what HE said;

"You are Fearfully and Wonderfully put together
Mighty, Victorious, Tough, yet Gentle like leather

I made You First before the woman appeared
I gave you Authority to name creatures, and I didn't interfere

I have already placed the Right tools in your hands,
Now, go build on my Unfailing Love,
Because That's… the Power of the Presence of A Man."

The Power of Touch

GeNeise Fuller – Author/Poet

The Power of Touch
It can heal a broken heart or fulfill a desire
It can mend a relationship that's about to expire

It can cause One, to be restored to health
It can literally save a life from death

The Power of Touch can bring about hope
It can lift you from depression and cause you to cope

It has the power to save a newborn's life
It can cause One to soar to new heights

It's infectious, exhilarating, comforting, transforming
It's audacious, amazing, turns nights into mornings

It can be a smile, a word, a kiss, an embrace
And don't underestimate the part you can play

If you want to leave a legacy that will produce much
Start sowing Good seeds with The Power of Touch.

LET ME LOVE YOU RIGHT

GeNeise Fuller – Author/Poet

There is a way that seems right to us humans
But the end thereof is destruction
All I want to do is to Love You Right
Without Sin or Corruption

I know my body is not my own
I have been bought with a price
And yes, I'll boldly say it aloud
I've given my life to Jesus Christ

I ask of you, let me love you right
With Honor, Respect, and a Holy Union
I will esteem you high above others
I will value our sweet communion

I ask of you baby, let me love you right
Like Solomon's Songs and Ephesians 5
And with the Grace and Wisdom of God
We can keep our love alive!

I ask of you, let me Love You Right…

Happy Father's Day - Man of God
GeNeise Fuller – Author/Poet

I know that 1-day
Couldn't possibly display
All the sacrifices
You've had to make

You provided for your family
In good times and bad
You were there
During happy times and sad

Man of God,
I am so proud of you
For standing the test of time
When Real Fathers are few

You are to be celebrated
Every day of the year!
So, I thank you, Man of God
Thank you for being here.

SHE WOULD BE SO PROUD

GeNeise Fuller – Author/Poet

Nothing can replace the loss of a Mother
Whether husband, wife, sister, or brother

If you can imagine her peeking through the clouds
Seeing how you've matured, I think she would be proud

You are smart, intelligent, gentle and kind
I think she would be proud, knowing that you will be fine

Cherishing the memories you've shared on earth
I know she would be so proud, just like the day of your birth.

The Power of CHOICES

GeNeise Fuller – Author/Poet

They can determine how you Live
And determine how you Die
They can take you to the Lowest Low
Or soar you to the Highest High

It is the difference between poverty
And living a life of wealth
It is the difference between sickness
And living in health

Choices are made every day
At the 'drop of a hat'
Unfortunately, some of those choices
Cannot be taken back!

It is deeper than you may think
Because YOU get to choose
YOU decide if you will win
And YOU decide if you will lose

There are consequences and rewards
For the choices you make
And that all will depend
Upon the path you take

You can trust The Almighty
As you go about your day
His Wisdom and Knowledge
Will not lead you astray

Because His ways
Are so much higher than man,
He will **Always** have
The Perfect Plan

My Game Plan...

What does my present situation look like?

_____

_____

_____

_____

_____

_____

_____

_____

_____

_____

_____

What do I want my future to be like?

_____

_____

_____

_____

_____

_____

_____

_____

_____

_____

_____

_____

_____

_____

What is my plan to get there?

_____

_____

_____

_____

_____

_____

_____

_____

_____

_____

_____

_____

_____

The BAD

(adjective) Failing to reach an acceptable standard
Source: Merriam-webster.com

Where Are You?
(A Message to Dads)

GeNeise Fuller – Author/Poet

Everywhere I go, the story is the same
Single Mothers carrying the load, even through physical pain

There are all types of 'programs' trying to fill in the gap
But they will never take the place of children sitting in their Father's lap

I am crying out to you, daddies, to come back home
Our Mothers are struggling, because you've left them alone

Many of our children have not experienced family life with Mom and Dad
A single family has been the norm, because it was all that they had

Where are you daddies, where are you fathers, you are a **Vital** part of our lives
Our Mothers are struggling physically and financially, some are making great strives

I challenge you now, to take your rightful place
Be a Man of Standard, of Family, of Grace

Daddies, you are The Answer to the gap in our families and homes
I beg you, rise to the occasion and don't leave another Mother alone!

Where Are They?
(Part 2 Message to Daddies)
GeNeise Fuller – Author/Poet

There is another trend
That should have been so obvious to me
Dads Missing in Action
When it comes to their family

Not only girls and boys;
The faces of a little child
I'm talking grown Men and Women
Who hasn't seen daddy in a while!

For some who do not know
Who their daddies are
Still struggle with unresolved issues
And fighting a silent war

I want to make it clear
I am not bashing the men
I'm addressing a Real problem
That's happening again and again

I just witnessed hurt and pain
In a young woman's voice
Telling how her childhood
Affected her choice

The closeness she so wants
Now, with her Dad
Is blocked by unforgiveness
And the struggles she had

It involves deep hurt
And Yes, even sin!

But can we all just take one step
Towards making amends?

In part, it's Generational
That has been passed down
But it doesn't have to continue
If we begin making a sound

A sound of Forgiveness
Can begin healing our hurt
And no one can point a finger
Because we've All have done some dirt

Too many times I've seen the face of pain
When Daddies aren't around
From kids and even adult children
Wounded, rejected and bound

Nothing will be resolved
If we choose Not to forgive
It might be hard at first, but it's worth it
If in Peace, we want to LIVE!

You see me, As a Strong Black Woman

GeNeise Fuller – Author/Poet

You see me as a strong black woman
But let me tell you how I got this way
From the time I was a little child
I've had to step-up to the plate

Life never came easy for me
I've always worked hard for what I got
Now, you see me as a strong black woman
And you think, a man? She need not.

I've seen down through generations
Black women had to be The Head
Though many, not wanting to be,
Had to survive or they would be dead

So, men, please don't see us as a threat
We want so… strongly for you to take The Lead!
Remember, you were created to be The Head
In part, we were created to birth the seed

Now, don't get it twisted,
I am not saying this is All to it
I'm saying let's come together,
With God as OUR head, we can do it!

We can help each other rise above the struggles
We can help each other love one another
And when you see me as a strong black woman,
You can see me standing beside my brother!

What happened to You?
GeNeise Fuller – Author-Poet

When you were down on your luck and didn't know what to do
Didn't know where to turn, **I** was there for you!

With words of encouragement and 'other' deeds too
To nourish and care until you saw your way through.

During such times, in need of help myself
Wanting to lean, but you had already left.

What happened to you, during my time of trouble?
Instead of comfort and security, your actions became subtle.

What happened to you? I thought you had my back
To be there for me, when the odds were stacked.

I thought we had a bond that was solid and strong
Now I must admit that I was wrong.

But, in the midst, I found a true friend
One that will stay until the very end.

He is my comfort, my security in time of need
My way maker, my Savior, my prayers He heeds.

What happened to you? It doesn't matter anymore
Because I am better off now, than I were before!

Let My Sister Go!
GeNeise Fuller – Author/Poet

My heart is saddened by the stories
I hear my sisters' tell
How their "covenant" partner rule their lives
And no freedom to be themselves

These ladies are 'Saved' and Love The Lord
But apparently their spouses are not
So, I'm trying to understand, how man got the upper hand
And settled in that spot?

Granted, God called man to be the head
Like Christ is over the church
He didn't call him to rule by abuse or fear
That is just too much!

The years I've lived I have seen
The decline in Women's respect
From Rappers taking their shot at us
Now the husbands! What the heck?

I've heard stories of my sisters in relationships
Where it wasn't their "covenant" spouse
I wanted to say, you don't have to take this
Get up and get out of the house!

To All of my sisters I want to say
My Love and Prayers are with you
I cannot say what I would do
If I was in your shoes

I can say this, You are soo valuable!
You are a Masterpiece!
No one has the right to abuse you in Any way
And this type of control has to cease!

You were created for Greatness
God hasn't changed His mind on that
I pray you find your voice of freedom
Because you're definitely Not a doormat!

And Now, You Wanna Come Back?

GeNeise Fuller – Author/Poet

A long time ago
When I was yours, and you were mine
The things you did weren't so kind.

The emotional and physical abuse I endured
From your mouth and hands
You haven't forgotten. I'm assured.

You had your fun
With this one and that.
You boldly did 'your thing'
You gave me No respect!

Now that life has thrown you a curve
You're all out of options
While my life has surged.

I have no ill feelings
You're forgiven for all that smack.
But one thing is for certain
I don't want you back!

I love the path
Where God is taking me.
Why would I choose bondage?
When HE has set me Free!

So keep moving farther
I pray the best for you.
I have a New beginning
Because that old life, I'm through!

Who Gave You the Right?!

GeNeise Fuller – Author/Poet

Who gave you the right, to take My life?
How dare you believe, that I wasn't Royalty
By the way you treated me!

Did you ever stop to think
That we weren't meant to be
And all you had to do
Was walk away in Peace?

Who gave you the right, to take My life;
When my destiny wasn't complete?
Now that I'm gone, I hope your heart of stone
Has led you to drop to your knees!

To deal with your issues that led me here,
And ask God to forgive.
Heaven knows the vicious cycle has to end,
So that Others can Live.

Who gave you the right, to take My life;
And then remain the same?
Be careful if you thought you got away
Because Payback can be a Boomerang!

The Power of Touch (the Other side)

GeNeise Fuller – Author/Poet

There is another side to the power of touch
It's something that's not talked about much

It can turn good into bad
It can make happy moments sad

It can steal the innocence of a little child
Turn purity into vile

It can violate with an unwanted advance
Cause the abused Not to take a stance

It can manifest in a physical, mental, or visual way
Emotional, psychological, or philosophical state

However, the case, you've got to stay alert
Because the Other side of touch, can harvest years of hurt.

REALLY???

GeNeise Fuller – Author/Poet

We say, stop the violence;
Don't kill anymore!
Yet we set our eyes
Before an open door.

Corrupt music, video games,
To the shows seen on TV;
It does have a <u>profound</u> effect
Even if you don't agree!

Evil, Murder,
Pornography and rape;
Soap opera's deception,
Lust and hate.

You wonder why it's raging
In our streets and homes?
It's because families
Have been left alone.

We want D.C.
To fund our bill.
By now you should know
It's not a magic pill.

Get informed
From more than just one source.
Think for yourself,
You have a voice.

Change will not happen
Until you commit;
To start charity at home
Then, you can make it legit.

If Black Lives Matter

GeNeise Fuller – Author/Poet

What I am about to say
May upset many.
But I promise, my intent
Is not to offend any.

I have burning questions
That is reflecting what I see.
And IF you have the answers
Please, explain it to me.

If black lives matter
Why can't we teach it to our men;
To save them from an early grave
Or a trip to the 'Pen'?

If black lives matter
Why can't we teach our girls;
To realize the life they may carry
Could one day change this world?

If black lives matter,
Why do we destroy our <u>own</u> businesses?
We say it's in the name of Justice.
Come on, you've got to be kidding me!

If we're going to talk the talk
About black lives matter;
Let us walk the walk,
And start working to do better.

If black lives matter
Then let's teach Our race.
Because, unless We really Value each other
These words could possibly be a waste.

My Game Plan...

What 1 bad habit I can work on now and how?

_____

_____

_____

_____

_____

_____

_____

_____

_____

_____

_____

3 ways I will show kindness to a Special Lady.

ALL of my children will know <u>daily</u> they are Loved by their Daddy.

By Hugs? By Calls/Texts? Other? (Explain)

_____

_____

_____

_____

_____

_____

_____

_____

_____

_____

_____

_____

_____

The BROKEN

(top definition) **Something that needs to be fixed**

Source: Urbandictionary.com

Who, will MENtor them?

GeNeise Fuller – Author/Poet

To tell you the truth
I'm not sure where to start.
This frustration of not understanding
Is weighing on my heart.

As I try to explain it
Please don't take offense.
This is a subject
That may cause you to tense.

I'm talking about the Men
Who hasn't a clue of being 'The Head'!
Because he hasn't been adequately Mentored,
He depends upon the woman instead.

I am all for doing my part
In helping out sometimes.
But certain responsibilities
Just shouldn't be mine!

There are Real Men Mentors
Who's been trained by the Best.
All it takes is humility
And your willingness.

Our generation has gone too long
Without a dominant Presence of Real Men.
They're either in prison, on drug, homeless
Or, one has killed another one, again!

I'm speaking of what I've observed
And much of what I've lived through.
No, I don't have all the answers
To tell you what to do.

I know it is a vicious cycle
And it doesn't have to be.
But change can start by dropping your pride
And sitting at a Real MENtor's feet.

© *(MENtor - MEN Training On Righteousness)

Save Our Men
GeNeise Fuller – Author/Poet

I pulled up at my bank and just next door
I can see the ABC Store.

So many men going in and out!
On their faces are hard times and distraught.

The surrounding areas are filled with my kind
My race, my struggles, that weren't left behind.

I'm sitting here wondering what can be done
To help eliminate the despair and break this bond!

Men relate to men is what I have been told
But sometimes a woman's touch can help a hurting soul.

I am writing because I am seeking for help
For answers, solutions, that next step!

To save our men and give them real hope
Tools of Life to help them cope

As I'm sitting here, a huge truck has just pulled up
Filled with more of the ABC stuff!

It is a vicious cycle that I know
But I'm a firm believer; we don't have to take no 'mo'!

Can somebody stand with me to make a difference today?
It's not too late to help our brothers seek a better way. ♥©

Why Didn't He Leave?
GeNeise Fuller – Author/Poet

I am staring at my brother lying in a hospital bed
With machines and tubes from his feet to head.

What happened to put him in that state?
Apparently, when Medics arrived it was already too late.

He coded twice, then was revived
And that gave us time to sit by his bedside.

He spoke not a word, nor opened his eyes.
But when his tears often appeared, it kept our hope alive.

Five days later, he gave up the ghost.
But what I learned from years earlier bothered me the most!

The hurt, pain, and neglect that my brother went through
All for the sake of Love, from his point of view.

Were there warning signs saying, 'get out while you can'!?
But no, not my brother, he wanted to be a Real man.

To help those who couldn't help themselves
All the while his life was just pure hell!

He wasn't treated right; and I know we have choices.
I guess he felt stuck in a barrage of voices.

I cannot ask him, why didn't you leave?
I can only say for my life, I will try to take heed.

To not be manipulated or controlled by 'man' *
But to yield my life into The Master's hand.

Witness after witness testified of my brother's good deeds.
I am thankful for that because he helped many in need.

I only wished that the Good Deeds were returned back to him
Then maybe today would be one of joy, and not one of grim!

RIP,
Douglas 'Peanut' Houston, my brother

* man meaning - mankind, human beings

Beneath the Smile

GeNeise Fuller – Author/Poet

Things appear to be Great!
The Blessings seem to flow.
But beneath the smile
No one can know.

The pain I feel inside
When life doesn't seem fair.
While beneath the beautiful smile
Crying, wondering, does anyone care?

Who do I run to
When the hurt is so strong?
Who will not judge me
When I want to do wrong?

Are you that Trusted friend
That will Pray me through?
Are you the stranger on the Prayer-line
When there's no one else to turn to?

I can hear you saying, hey
You can always go to God!
Yes, this I know is true.
But let me share Another part.

When you are hurting and in pain
Where are the 'people' who care;
One you can touch, embrace,
That is physically there?

God uses mankind
To show His Awesome Love.
He won't literally come down
From His home above.

We have to be His voice
His hands and his feet.
We must become sensitive
To our brothers and sisters' needs.

So many are hurting
Beneath that beautiful smile!
And if we're prayerful and alert
We can help make their life worthwhile.

UnWanted Child
GeNeise Fuller – Author/Poet

Now that I am a grown-up
And has experienced life for awhile
I realize more and more
That **I** was an unwanted child!

Where is my Dad?
As an adult, I began to ask?
But as a child
That thought wasn't a task.

I had a Mom
Who was there all the time
Taking care of business
Making the family shine.

It didn't occur me until later
There, should have been my Dad!
Loving on us, caring for us
Giving All that he had.

But, the day came when,
I began my search
To find what was Rightfully mine
My Dad, whom I was void of touch.

When I found him, I saw
He also, was happy to see me!
But the union didn't last
Because 'Issues' didn't allow it to be.

Today, my eyes became open
That I was an Unwanted child.
My Dad left my Mom
He never looked back or picked up to dial.

I can't say it doesn't hurt
Even though my Heavenly Father cares.
But knowing that my natural father
At least for me, he wasn't there.

Am I bitter about it?
No, I am not.
I just want to tell him
He missed out on a lot!

I wish he had been there
When I was in school.
To help with my homework
I know he would have made it smooth.

I wish he had been there
When I walked across the stage.
I know he would have been rootin'
Shouting, that's my babe!

I wish he had been there
To talk to me about 'crazy' boys!
I wish he'd been there on holidays
Especially, Us playing with my Christmas toys.

Dad, I miss you
Wherever you are!
I wished I was wanted
Then maybe you wouldn't be afar.

God, will You talk to my daddy for me?

GeNeise Fuller – Author/Poet

God,
Will you talk to my daddy for me?
Will you tell him,
I miss him terribly?

I haven't seen him
In a long, long time.
Will you ask him,
Am I on his mind?

God,
Will you talk to my daddy for me?
Tell him my heart aches;
Because it's him I long to see.

Can you tell him that I love him,
And wish I could see his face;
Or hear his voice,
Or receive a loving embrace?

Can you tell him,
He's in my thoughts, my dreams and my prayers;
And my empty arms are open,
To welcome and let him know I'll forever care?

God, can You talk to my daddy for me?

FED UP!!!
GeNeise Fuller – Author/Poet

Have you ever felt you were the tail and not the head?
Or, instead of being a blessing, you were the one begging for bread?

Have you tried so hard to live life right?
Only to feel like you were losing the fight?

You Knew God had blessed you with special talents and gifts.
But everywhere you turned, no one seemed to give You a lift!

You're always working overtime trying to hold on to your home.
Doesn't feel like the struggle is over. It's like you're out there on your own!

You Know you've been a blessing in the lives of many.
But when You are in need, there aren't any!

I think 'Fed-up' is a place where quite a few have been.
And if you haven't… I say, live on my friend! ♥©

Black Men DO Cry

GeNeise Fuller – Author/Poet

With the struggles that our black men had to endure
From Africa to America wasn't easy, I'm sure!

Through the brutal era of slavery
To the Civil Rights March
Believing one day justice will come
Keeping the Faith was sometimes hard.

When I look at our black men today
Most are struggling with a different kind of fray
With prison, unemployment, homelessness, and drugs
I realized the Power of a Mother's hug!

Black Men DO Cry
When they hear the right words.
Like, "I am Proud of You! I believe in You!"
Words, some Never heard!

Like, "You are a Great Father,
Son, or Friend
Or, I've got your back, baby
I am with You 'till the end!"

Black Men DO Cry.
It's not always tears of sorrow.
Encourage a black man today
Don't wait 'till tomorrow!

Encouraging the Man I Love
GeNeise Fuller – Author/Poet

A look of hopelessness I see upon your face
Wondering how will we make it. I say, with God's Grace.

You are my love, be assured of that
I love you with All my heart, and that's a fact!

We are going to make it, no matter how it may look
God Almighty is our source and we believe in HIS Book.

Try not to stress about what is in front of you
You have my love and support. I appreciate All you do!

Just keep your head up. We are coming out, I know
This is just temporary. Soon, it will blow.

I am proud of you. You work hard to care for us.
Baby, I am right by your side, together with Christ, we can trust…

That He has our lives in the palm of His hands
He will not be out-done; no, not by Any man!

If we put our trust and hope in Him
He will lift us out of this situation that seems dimmed.

Keep your head up high baby; the Lord is on our side
He is Jehovah Jireh, our Provider.
He is the God that Never lied!

Lord, Teach him How to Love Me

GeNeise Fuller – Author/Poet

You are the creator of man
You've made him to be The Head.
Lord, teach him how to love me
The way Your Word said.

I will submit
I will Honor and Respect.
Lord, teach him how to love me
A love he won't regret!

And when he loves his body
As he loves himself,
Then I know he can love Me
Like No One Else!

My Game Plan...

Who are my Mentors?

Who am I Mentoring?

_____

_____

_____

_____

_____

_____

_____

_____

_____

_____

_____

_____

_____

_____

_____

_____

How am I Impacted by either one?

_____

_____

_____

_____

_____

_____

_____

_____

_____

_____

_____

_____

_____

_____

The SOLUTION?

(noun) A means of solving a problem...
Source: Google.com

But what about, your word?
GeNeise Fuller – Author/Poet

Talk is cheap; anyone can speak!
Where is the proof, when it's time to produce?

I am told your word is your bond.
But some people use it as a con.

Think before you speak. Do what you say you'll do.
Not only does it affect others but it also affects you.

When it is time to step up to the plate
Do your part. Don't hesitate!

You **know** someone is counting on you.
You gave them your word; now make it true.

Excuses yes, we're so quick to use.
Keep them to yourself because I am not amused!

Start setting the pace for Integrity.
Because if you were in my shoes, I'm sure you'd agree;

That in the final analysis the job ***still*** has to be done.
And without back-up plans, you could be singing ***sad*** songs.

It's Hell being a Trailblazer!
GeNeise Fuller – Author/Poet

(Setting the pace is not an easy fate)

If you are a 1st born, "out of the box" thinker
or "go against the grain"?
Suit up, prepare for the fight,
get ready for the pain!

When your thoughts and ideas
has never been heard or done;
Don't be surprise that the number of people cheering,
Is only **one**!

There is always a process
before you hit the scene;
Be patient and learn it
because this world can be mean.

Even the strongest believer
sometimes breaks down.
But when you know your purpose,
negativity can't stay around.

There will always be forces
assigned to make you quit,
To shame you, even bully you,
to make you doubt your pick!

The fact that you're a trailblazer
will involve a certain amount of risk.
But if you're willing to step out and make a difference
Then your purpose, you won't miss.

Yes, the journey sometimes gets hard;
but you have to BREAK through.
And because You Are a Trailblazer,
That is what You Do!

The Power of YOU!
GeNeise Fuller – Author/Poet

Yes You, who are fearfully **and** wonderfully made
From the dust of the earth then Heavenly raised.

Created for purpose by design
to make an impact in this Lifetime.

You have the Seed of Greatness inside of You!
To help you with what You were destined to do.

If you're in that state where you don't have a clue
Let me continue with The Power of You.

Before you were even thought of on Earth
God had already planned your birth.

Let me tell you what The Father said about you
"You are More than a Conqueror an Overcomer", it's true!

"You are a Chosen Generation, An Ambassador of Light
You're protected by His Blood and healed by His stripes!"

You're so loved by The Father,
That He's given you keys to His home.
And He sent you a Savior and Comforter
So, you won't ever be alone.

He gives you strength to do all things if you just believe
Then He backs it up by saying, "I'll supply All your needs."

I tell ya, He believes in The Power of You!
It doesn't matter about the negative voices,
His Voice is The Only Truth!

So, rise up, go forward; know that this is your time!
He's already given you the power of love,
NOT fear, and a sound mind!

To do those things He's prompting you to do
And to never lose sight in The Power of You!

Will You be THE One?

GeNeise Fuller – Author/Poet

Why do you have to be like someone else?
Why can't you think for yourself?

If their pants drag down to the ground;
Why can't you be **the** One whose mind is sound?

If they want to do drugs and create violence in the streets;
Why can't you be **the** One, who says hey, that's not for me?

If temper flares to the point where men chooses to kill a brother;
Why can't you be **the** One who says, listen man, Not another!?

When will it stop? When will someone step up to the plate!?
When will strong role models come forward before it's too late?

When will someone say, I have a mind of **My** own?
And I will **not** be led to do wrong!

Though I may not get it right every time;
But I am determined to make *my life shine*!

… Will You be **the** One?

It Only Takes One
GeNeise Fuller – Author/Poet

I heard a young man give a powerful speech.
He talked about a mentor who changed his destiny.

He said when they met their ages were only 3 years apart.
But the wisdom from his mouth became the direction for his heart.

He kept repeating over and over, "It Only Takes One".
That's when I began to think about 'the Son'.

If we would only take the time to tell just one, about 'The Christ'
Imagine what that would do, to impact a person's life!

I <u>WILL</u> make a difference in the life of someone else!
And I'll esteem them higher than I do myself.

It only takes one to lend a helping hand.
To give a smile, a kind word to a fellow man.

It doesn't take a lot to get the job done.
If you're willing to submit, it only takes One!

The Power of Influence

GeNeise Fuller – Author/Poet

It can cause weak minds to go astray
Or persuade just One not to go that way

It can cause a group to bully One
Or persuade One to look to The SON

It can cause a culture to defy what is right
To compromise morals no matter the plight

The Power of Influence presents itself everyday
And only You can decide what path you will take

Wide is the gate that leads to destruction
Narrow is the way you want to choose
It may feel like you're in a 'no-win' situation
But with God's Power of Influence, you will never loose.

EXCUSES
GeNeise Fuller – Author/Poet

Excuses, excuses, you hear them everyday
Take your excuses and throw them away!

There are New things God wants to do
But your Old way of thinking will hinder you.

If you're a new creature in Christ, don't you forget
He has promises for you that haven't been fulfilled yet!

Renew your mind and cast your care
He'll show you signs that you're on your way there.

You have to expect. You have to believe.
You have to know that you will succeed!

If you don't let excuses creep back in
You will have the Victory because in Him, You Win! ❤️©

I'll Make it Worth Your Time
GeNeise Fuller – Author/Poet

If you wake up in a 'funk'
with complaining on your mind
Come to the 'Prayer Closet',
I'll make it worth your time.

If you dare to think,
of Not putting Me first
Rethink again,
I will make it your worth!

I have answers for you,
to take the struggle away.
I have secrets and nuggets,
especially for You today.

I have the Riches you need
and many successful tools.
I have the Wisdom that goes with it
So you won't look like a fool!

Put Me first in your day,
no greater Love treasure you will find
If you would do that, I promise,
I'll make it worth your time!
(Wow God!)

Prayer for Direction
GeNeise Fuller – Author/Poet

Father, there are some decisions
I really have to make.
And I need your guidance
on which direction to take.

At this point I am not sure
What to do
I ask for your Wisdom
on the right path to choose.

I draw close to Your Presence
and I incline my spiritual ear.
Because I want to make sure
of every word I hear.

I trust you Father
as I submit to You in prayer.
Thank You for Your guidance
And for Always being there.

I Love You Father….

My Game Plan...

Tools I need to be that Powerful MAN

_____

_____

_____

_____

_____

_____

_____

_____

_____

_____

_____

_____

Where will I go to get them?

What am I waiting on?

_____

_____

_____

_____

_____

_____

_____

_____

_____

_____

_____

GO! And be ALL that God has CALLED You to be!

THE
POWER
OF A MAN

The AFTERWORD

Dear Powerful Man,
I pray this book was a blessing to you.
I am honored to share my thoughts through Poetry of how much I believe in the Power of A Man!
In the words of King David, Old Testament Bible, "You are Fearfully and Wonderfully made." Psalm 139:14
You are somebody my friend, because God don't make no junk!
I heard Jeff Kemp, former NFL Quarterback, say: "God doesn't make anything but Excellence."

We all have made mistakes and more than likely, will again. The beautiful thing about it is that, we have a Heavenly Father, who sent His Only Son to die for those mistakes. The Son (didn't stay dead), reunited and sent from Heaven the Holy Spirit to lead, guide, and help us (without condemnation!) live a life of freedom, love, and peace!

If you haven't already invited Him into your heart, take a moment right now and do so. If you have strayed away, come back to Him. He stands ready with open arms to love you back to Life!
HE is the God that Heals and Forgives. Let Him in TODAY.

Pray this: Dear Heavenly Father, I acknowledge my sin and mistakes to You. Forgive me and receive me as Your son. I believe in the birth, death, and resurrection of your son, Jesus Christ. Thank you for Saving me! Now lead and guide me according to Your perfect Will. Amen.

(If you prayed this prayer, let us know. We want to welcome and celebrate You into the family of God. Email, **'I'm In!'** to: info@thepowerofaman.com).

Your little sister in Christ,
- GeNeise -

The AUTHOR

Who is GeNeise Fuller aka 'Lady Ge'?

She is President/CEO of **A C C E S S** Organization, Inc.
An **S.E.C**. Company that is **S**aving, **E**mpowering & **C**elebrating Lives.
This full-time Entrepreneur wears many hats.

- She is a Best-selling Author, Speaker, Dance and Personal Coach.

- She is Host of Thirsty Thursday LIVE; a private FB broadcast that empowers ladies with Real and thought-provoking topics.

- Her *GeNeise* Ink♥ Brand is an E-commerce store with products and custom items designed to further empower her audience.

- Look for her Podcast coming soon, entitled, RT {RealTalk} with Lady Ge'.

- Bottom line, with every gift and talent she posses, GeNeise is a woman determined to continue to be a Strong Advocate in **S**aving Children's Lives (especially those exposed to secondhand smoke), **E**mpowering 'Awesome' Ladies (from hurting to healed) and **C**elebrating Families (starting with Honoring Men as head)!

She is available to speak at men and/or women conferences and events!
For Bookings, email: **geneiseink@gmail.com**
Subject: Booking

www.ingramcontent.com/pod-product-compliance
Lightning Source LLC
Chambersburg PA
CBHW042332150426
43194CB00001B/32